Elvis

I can read the Speed sou

I can read the Green words.

I can read the Red words.

I can read the story.

I can answer the questions about the story.

I can read the Speed words.

Say the Speed sounds

Consonants

Ask your child to say the sounds (not the letter names) clearly and quickly, in and out of order. Make sure he or she does not add 'uh' to the end of the sounds, e.g. 'f' not 'fuh'.

f	l ll	m	n	r	s ss	v	z	sh	th	ng nk

b	c k ck	d	g	h	j	p	qu	t	w	x	y	ch

Each box contains one sound.

Vowels

Ask your child to say each vowel sound and then the word, e.g. 'a', 'at'.

at	hen	in	on	up	day	see	high	blow	zoo

Read the Green words

*For each word ask your child to read the separate sounds, e.g. 't-a-p',
'b-l-a-ck' and then blend the sounds together to make the word, e.g. 'tap',
'black'. Sometimes one sound is represented by more than one letter,
e.g. 'ng', 'sh', 'ck'. These are underlined.*

tap   am   elf   sa<u>ng</u>   mend   red

hat   ca<u>sh</u>   box   dre<u>ss</u>   pi<u>nk</u>

bla<u>ck</u>   do<u>ll</u>   big   his   pi<u>ng</u>

Ask your child to read the word in syllables.

El`vis → Elvis

Ask your child to read the root word first and then the word with the ending.

mend → mendi<u>ng</u>   thi<u>ng</u> → <u>th</u>i<u>ng</u>s
imp → imps   do<u>ll</u> → do<u>ll</u>s

Read the Red words

*Red words don't sound like they look. Read the words out to your child.
Explain that he or she will have to stop and think about how to say the
red words in the story.*

I   y<u>ou</u>   <u>the</u>   my   wand

Elvis

Introduction

Meet an elf called Elvis. Most elves mend shoes, but this elf will mend anything. Even ... well, let's find out.

Elvis is an elf.

His job is mending things.

Tap! Tap! Tap!

Tap! Tap!

"I am Elvis the elf!"
Elvis sang.

"I can mend
the witch's wand . . ."

Tap tap

Ping!

"I can mend
the imp's red hat . . ."

Stitch stitch

Ping!

"I can mend the king's big black cash box ..."

Tap tap

Ping!

"I can mend the doll's pink dress . . ."

Stitch stitch

Ping!

"Can you mend my socks?"

Elvis sang, "I am Elvis the elf!

I can mend a wand, a hat . . .

a box,

a dress . . .

. . . and, yes, I can mend socks!"

Questions to talk about

Ask your child:

Page 6:   *What is Elvis' job?*

Page 8:   *What does Elvis sing as he mends?*

Page 20: *List all the things Elvis has mended.*

Speed words

Ask your child to read the words across the rows, down the columns and in and out of order, clearly and quickly.

tap	mend	sang	elf	red
hat	cash	thing	box	my
doll	the	dress	you	pink
black	doll	big	I	mending